© 2022 Experiments in Fiction.

Jeff Flesch
Nature Speaks of Love and Sorrow

All rights reserved. No part of this publication may be reproduced, stored in a retrieval system or transmited in any form or by any means, electronic, mechanical, photocopying, recording or otherwise without the prior permission of the publisher or the author of the relevant work who retains the copyright of his work in accordance with the provisions of the Copyright, Designs and Patents Act 1988 or under the terms of any license permitting limited copying issued by the Copyright Licensing Agency.

ISBN: 978-1-7397577-5-5

Jeff Flesch

**NATURE SPEAKS
OF LOVE AND SORROW**

Experiments in Fiction

NATURE SPEAKS

of Love and Sorrow

Jeff Flesch

FOR MY FAMILY AND FRIENDS.
I LOVE YOU.

My Dearest Readers

The book you now hold in your hands was a labor of love. My love for everyone and everything on this beautiful planet. The collection herein is full of my contemplations on life, and our connections to nature.

As a child, I loved to be outdoors and to use my imagination to create worlds unseen to everyone but me. I believe Maya Angelou describes the sentiment of the unseen best, "Faith is the evidence of the unseen". Indeed, faith is also believing in ourselves, our imagination, and our unique creative potential.

The beauty of poetry is that I now get to share my imagination with you.

I find great resonance in nature, and in my connections with everyone I know, all of whom have touched my heart in some way.

On each page of this book is my heart and soul. A heart and soul that are open to both the love and the sorrow life has given me.

I thank you for being a part of my journey. A journey of self-discovery and self-examination. One that has been a blessing to me each day.

All my love and blessings,

Jeff Flesch

Corvallis, Oregon June 12, 2022

"Earth laughs in flowers."

—Ralph Waldo Emerson

"Forget not that the earth delights to feel your bare feet and the winds long to play with your hair."

—Khalil Gibran

"To make a prairie it takes a clover and one bee,
One clover, and a bee,
And revery.
The revery alone will do,
If bees are few."

—Emily Dickinson

Contents

Neutral Stances	*15*
Hearth and Home	*16*
Oak Trees	*17*
Mountains Gold	*18*
Slow-Motion Moments	*20*
Dream Sky	*21*
Ocean and Sand	*22*
Love's Trials	*23*
Blueberry Tree	*24*
Blackberry Brambles	*25*
Golden Sunshine	*26*
Mango Trees	*27*
Cascading Water	*28*
Cosmic Arts	*29*
Lavender Sheds	*30*
Soft and Cherished	*31*
Limbs and Leaves	*32*
Apples Intoned	*33*
Blooming Tears	*34*
Birds and Stone	*35*
Earth's Crust	*36*
Self-Bloom	*37*
Willow Trees	*38*

Daisies Planted	39
Love's Hourglass	40
Golden Haze	41
Needle and Thread	42
Seas and Skies	43
Strident Tides	44
Cherry Trees	45
Cherries Glisten	46
Blue Kiss	47
Orange Sky	48
A Deluge	49
Watered Veins	50
Mystical Rain	51
Weaved Interlude	52
Lemons and Limes	53
Butterfly Love	54
The Pencil	55
A Trickle Mist	56
A Nostalgic Place	57
The Sweetest Lullaby	58
Sea and Spirit	59
Green Leaves	60
Winter Garden	62
Veins Full of Sorrow	63
Broken Dreams	64
The Ocean's Rocks	66
Winds of Time	67
Moments Grasped	68

Neutral Stances

dreams supplanted
by neutral stances

always awake me in the night
while anxieties are up, have taken flight

into the heart
of the mysteries, they call to me
when time is not
in sight

I cannot rely
upon the soundness of the rain
it's paramount for me to remain
calm

yet, their faces still come to me in dreams
and all I want to do is flee

this life for another
but knowing all the silliness, why bother?

until love comes to me in brilliant shades and hues
and colors magical supplant the nakedness at noon:

while I lean into the love I feel for you

Hearth and Home

dreams catch my eye
a tangled weave defined

by the sight
of you near me until the end of time

I rely

upon a whisper in the wind
calling to me, the road narrow and thin

crumbly too, in places soft with the paleness of your skin

I wonder

about the love within my heart
as relations of the past come on

while I depart

in mist and stone
carrying me toward your hearth and home

Oak Trees

the oak trees, tall
their branches a reflection of the sea

resemble the veins of my heart
or lines of the part

you played, when young
and carefree

reminding me

of our hiding place: a hollowed-out tree
where a nest of care was kept

unseen, together
we

awaited the return of the stars, in blankets
warm and cool

covering a heart much bigger than the moon

Mountains Gold

Live.

the life you've always dreamed of
like the railway
you traveled when you were young

Stop.

now and again
to relish all the love and hope you feel
and remember

the flowers growing from seeds
into the hands of your
beloved

as they depart
this plane for another mystery
unknown, and known
and

Breathe.

into the sand, salt, stone
and mortified flesh of the bone

realizing that each and every gift
of nature's aspects is ours
to behold

while we learn more
about the manifestations atop the mountains

of gold

Slow-Motion Moments

I walk through the forest
watching the flowers bloom, while listening

to the breeze

it always seems
like an avalanche of thoughts pervade me

in moments of silence, while

flowers slowly open to the sun, and
leaves dance in the air

falling from the canopy above, for
it is in these slow-motion moments where

I learn more about the truth of our love

Dream Sky

two steps, then three, recall to me

a blanket seen beneath the earth

covering the light, while illuminating
the inner night

a place of magic, dwelling like a house
spent in the summer months all of a drought

baked and cracked
while not knowing completely

nevertheless, I know
all is as it should be

continuing
to run free

a dream the size of the sky, within me

Ocean and Sand

the ocean and sand
put me in mind of the taste of your lips
and the breath

of your dew-laden kisses

given to me one at a time, knowing
the riddle of humankind

was hard for me to understand

a mystery
drawn from the petals and fragrance
of your soul

dividing my world into two unknowns
living amongst my deep and drawn-out sorrow

which seeps into the sand
one granule at a time

while you and I

await the next sunrise

Love's Trials

I'm off the hook, relating a love
that's traveled a thousand miles

through pain and suffering, experienced
through many trials

dangling in mid-air, I come up
casting a comparative stare

towards the moon

I see you. Do you see me too?

I wonder
about the nature of being
as I contemplate the distance between myself

and this vision of you I'm seeing

Blueberry Tree

a land of roses bending over the sky
reminds me

of long-lost childhood times

watching vines grow across walls
while I waited for love to blaze from fiery coals

smoke billowing up, and
out over the night

a steely determination we did find

in the heart of the blueberry tree
whose fragrance, and presence always consoled me

picking a berry out of the line
in reverence and remembrance of the love
gifted to us throughout these wondrous times

Blackberry Brambles

through the vines of blackberry brambles
I grew up

learning to love
although there wasn't much

while in the sky, I always did reside

learning from those around me, taught with
patience and pride

of life's myriad scales and trials
though sometimes I would fail

just like a seedling starting out, I pushed my way up
through the ground

a little at a time, reaching
looking around

at all the beauty I had found

Golden Sunshine

living, loving, and tired with sunburned skin
I remember

the loss at the end of the twine herein

grasping, and settling back

I relax

breathing into the confusion
while watching daisies dance around my ankles

I resonate in
the weave around the inside

as I let go of the last time
we said goodbye, and

breathe into the summer's golden sunshine

Mango Trees

bricks made of mud, salt, and water
cast to me

a shadow

of a crestfallen star, nested in the
moon's heart

which speaks to me when blue, relating troubles

while mirroring a restlessness
a resonance of truth

of a love residing

within the mango trees, and other flora that
we see

reflecting all the beauty that is you and me

Cascading Water

I engrave your name across my heart
with words that come to me when lost

in troubled parts

while dances of cascading water
lure me in
to a love that sits on this side of the moon

it stands the test of time
even when there's so much stress and turmoil
felt within

pausing to breathe
fireflies come in a whisper, a wide grin

cascades over the clouds, revealing
the stars' hearts

tangled, and woven together just right
until we finally choose to depart

as our love takes flight

Cosmic Arts

birds live under my skin
wallowing in water, shallow and thin

I make do
with a smile, benign

while contemplating all the many mysteries hidden
inside of dreams and thoughts unbidden

have you ever tried to catch a glance of heaven?

look around you now, and watch

as the sun comes up inside your heart
shining on everything within range of the cosmic arts

Lavender Sheds

blues remind me of you
while lavenders recall forgotten hues

imbued

with articles once definite, now lost

do you remember the days when the sun hid
inside the chamber of our hearts?

like an imagined crescendo
of mountain tops

wavering on the riverfront
embossed

with latitude, and longitude
and other attributes of time

masking ourselves
imagined, heart and mind

while love arose, with purpose
let us shine

Soft and Cherished

I take my time, and often confide

in my heart of hearts
a pure delight

finding the center
of a love both soft and cherished

as apples bow trees
know that you always have been true to me:

while lingering in the shade took shape
you always compensate

and show me the truth behind the curtain
of the love we did create

Limbs and Leaves

I struggle to find you
it's as if the vapor of your essence was lost

inside the trunk of an old tree
stony and embossed

running my fingers over our names
I trade my stay

to enter into the hovel
we've now made

out of the love carved out of limbs and leaves
while nurturing our souls, we trade

the sun inside our hearts
for the remainder of our days

Apples Intoned

I want to find a way to dive into
your arms

while cherries grow fingers of discord

and
you make hope out of red apples intoned
with love, growing on vines

like a sun waiting for its time to shine

flowers bearing fruit of pain and hope
both

linger along my spine
as I enter a new aspect of space and time

Blooming Tears

gold folded end over end, tucked in
behind the necessity of our mutuality of kin

calls to mind butterflies in the summertime
and relations

we shared, and dwelt inside
while blooming tears both wet and dried

teaching me more than all the books
I've read in my past lives:

I wonder if we'll listen

moist and damp, I glisten
and radiate like a leaf in the dew
a pastime or two

takes me halfway home
where my hope continues to grow

Birds and Stone

I dream of birds and stone
they both remind me of my home

amongst the trees, with you and me
consigning clouds of cares and stars to

the breeze

I collect my tears, and walk with you
through my dreams

one moment, becomes the next, know that it is you
I'll never forget

while I contemplate the dream we kept

Earth's Crust

flower fields are found across the globe
a common place we call our home

growing from dust
on the surface of the earth's crust

we imagine a world where love lives at the center

removed from the shadowed world
we enter

you, me, and everyone else we see

a mirror stopping time
divining deeper into aspects of the common mind

Self-Bloom

I dance to the tune of the moon
learning more about nature

and the aspects

of self
hidden under the trees in bloom

they always call to me in the night
as love becomes more true

lingering
in the shadow of your darkness

I wonder about the light
inside the apple seeds
brought forth from that time

when two were divided through and through
knowing

that's usually when I call out to you

Willow Trees

I've traveled near and far
looking for love grown apart

riddled with ambiguity
there was always a sense of complacency

that happened when we last crossed
each other's path

I wonder at times if this romance will last

the test of time, like the burgeoning of April's
rain showers

a stormy dream cast
into the net of a love as tender
as the branches of the willow trees' last dance

Daisies Planted

love lives in the alley behind the shop
where the mystery stopped

and you entered my heart

walking within a dream
you came to meet me

in the courtyard of our life
before there were daisies planted in the garden

such a long way to travel with strife

lingering in the shade
the shadows did always play

with the wind, combined they set on us a grin

wide and deep
like the love we felt for each other within

Love's Hourglass

I find myself on a lonely
and desolate street

with streetlamps that illuminate my heart

and while I walk
I listen

to the breeze
wafting through the alleys of my mind

in time

while rivers of blood soak my feet
and I continue to dream

of you, resplendent and deep
thoughts

come to me at last
while I listen to your love pervade my soul
through the sands of time's bright hourglass

Golden Haze

the sea caresses me gently, while I
walk along the floor

finding so much to explore

sand sparkles like diamonds in the sky
reminding me

of the nature of the mind, a mirror wafting
in the breeze

a golden haze

trimmed of past experiences
which resonate with memories of you

I call out to the void
as my heart sinks below the surface

of the tide
please know, I will always abide

in our love clandestine

Needle and Thread

love leans into me
just like a piece of you

a memory
tasting like the afternoon sun

while I relish the fragrance of flowers
they come

to me

bright with emotion, and I feel
the soft breeze caressing my pores

did you know it was you lost in my prose?

alas, as the moments tick by
it is you I look for in the wind

while I needle the thread to weave our love within

Seas and Skies

thoughts of you
like an afternoon breeze
rush in so fast

silencing all others at long last

for love is hard to find
like opening an iron clasp

yet in you
there is respite from the storm

where trinkets sparkle in the sun
gloriously engraved upon my heart's stone

melting me down
one moment more

is all I ask

knowing deep down
it's you I've searched the seas and skies for

Strident Tides

I consider my life
a mystery of proportions

lived in long and strident tides related to
love's pale distortion

like the tree limbs, my fragments of being become thin

wafting in the evening breeze, between
the dew mist upon the changing hues
of your love

shining brightly like a pendant star
I reply to you:

'Say goodbye to me once more
but do not fear
I know I'll always hold you dear
our love is always near'

Cherry Trees

I look for you
high and low, my brow furrowed with
a sorrow all my own

my heart aches
for past mistakes, for each cherry on the tree
it takes

to conjure the magic of my heart
in place

a tide of emotions comes in waves and waves

as I say goodbye to you one last time
letting go of the feelings:

shy

yet not too much so
for my love must be known and shown

Cherries Glisten

cherries fall from the trees
they listen to me

glistening in the rain

as I dance through the trauma and pain

have you ever left the pain behind,
in search of some other state of mind?

I have too

it comes fast
when we realize love is all there is

ever was, or will be
a triumph over the past

reminding me to be present in the winds
of change, of all we've ever been

which tells us just as much

as the love which grows within the heart of trust

Blue Kiss

trusting instincts as they arise
I find common ground in the sunrise

it is a special time for me
wandering across this planet in a dream

of circumstances
while in search of past romances

and tales from all the books we've read

do we learn more from life than that which is in our heads?

I wonder about things like this
a common and in some ways trivial pursuit

while searching the earth over for you
and the kiss you last gave me under skies so blue

Orange Sky

orange is the color of the sky
and the image I find of you in the night

dancing before my mind
although I'm tired and weary

still I find in you delight

considering all the things you've done
like showing me how to become a man

while learning to let go of all my shame —
complacency

drops instead

letting love burn through the atmosphere inside my heart
and head

A Deluge

orange and yellow
remind me of a fever halo

or subtle mirage in the distance
while I wrestle with my existence

it's an interesting contemplation
even when fears materialize without insistence

malingering behind the sun
like time's effect, when all is said and done

a moment passes, and then two

while I sit and I listen
to the clouds bursting wide open:

a deluge, like the love I feel for you

Watered Veins

the rain splashes my soul
as my tears soak the soil

seeping into the detritus on the side of the hill
watching the sunrise
as my feelings swell with zeal

and with a vibrancy that's all their own

as a child
I always wondered why this might be so

did you know?

many people think it's all in their control
while love endures throughout the pain
we learn how to survive each day

giving back the love

watered within our veins

Mystical Rain

sometimes thoughts running free
present a problem for me

they disappear behind the clouds
part of a mystical rain shroud

that lingers
as I listen to the wind caress the chimes

and feelings called to mind
match wandering words
which gurgle, ink the page

and so relate an understanding which has stood the test of time

of all the love within my heart and mind

Weaved Interlude

flowers sit on top of the sunshine, and
therein lies

a multiplicity of conspired ties that bind

the heart and soul into one fully formed being
it's always you, in thought and in feeling

in the sun, the wind, and in the seas
toward the end of the dreamscape's thread

I pull on it lightly

and
as the needle goes through
we witness a weaved interlude

notes high and low, and in every part of the magic
in-between

and under the snow

don't you know, we always return the love we're shown

Lemons and Limes

I dream of lemons and limes
it's the scent that keeps me in line

watching them stock the shelves
brings back memories of a love that arose
above the clouds

dispersing my heart in one spell
shattering it into a thousand pearly raindrops

incandescent
and already shelved

like the lemons and limes I'm waiting to buy

with reminiscences, I bide my time

Butterfly Love

I rise from the ashes of past
circumstances

with a ladle of love in my right hand
and butterflies alighting on my left

thinking about the trees dwelling within me,
how they do always seem

lost in times of chaos, yet they
keep me warm

tangled emotions
cutting deep within, where love and pain
are perfect twins

and life is lived beneath the texture of your skin

The Pencil

there are lands in the sky
and in the words which we weave in the night

these textures and colors spring to mind again
reminding me of all the people I have known and been:

they live within me
even when they've passed into the light

a sparkle in my eye
which teaches me the magic of friendship
and of so much more besides

like the pencil I draw creating hearts
drawn from the love inside

A Trickle Mist

I reminisce over the dreams I've
kissed

as a trickle becomes a mist

thoughts of you are on the run
throughout my heart and mind
transporting me back to another time

when we watched the sunset behind the waves
and we learned how to touch each other
in that certain way

a day
lingers

as I whisper to the stars
a canopy of brilliance filters through

just like my memory of you

A Nostalgic Place

diamonds sparkle within my mind
like cherries and blueberries in the
summertime

a nostalgic place
made up of wheat fields

and
all of the dreams that you and I have held

since we were little
when escape into the expanse
seemed so real

stars offset by the brilliance of your smile
into my heart
you shine

holding me close
your breath enters my veins

and
pours promise of you into the center

for it is there
we now remember

The Sweetest Lullaby

the rain cascades like sheets of music

a stage like any other
filled with love
and the pain of one another

dreams fill my mind
bejeweled
I look to the sky

and find the sweetest lullaby

made of orange peels
and the limes I bought last week on sale

they float in the atmosphere
meandering between rocks
and points of light

racing toward a destiny predesigned
filled with the love from generations of time

Sea and Spirit

sand spills into my heart, each granule
made of time

a part of the fear left behind, yet it is
also part of the sea and spirit

a fairy tale —
clandestine

to know more, love more, and to leave
the rocks behind, shored

believing in the stars again
knowing

A grin.

expresses me, and the hell I've been
through

the unknown comes in waves now
showing more

while leaving me with a whisper
of love's rain, as it pours

Green Leaves

desperate skies
remind me of agonizing times

pebbles always underfoot, while salt
stings my eyes

always being told boys don't cry

pain is deep
into the atmosphere
it often creeps

along a line, just like the storms brewing
above an afternoon of calm —
divine

making a new start I resign the past,
being one with my heart —
I stand, steadfast

among the green leaves
which are now a part of me

like the stars in the sky
and the moon in my heart

trembling a vibrancy, both deep and broad

remembering the little boy within
now coming to the surface

letting love burn through

his purpose
now, just like a furnace

Winter Garden

I dig through my veins, like the pages
of a story, changed

through a subtle dance of pain

recollecting red leaves in the fall
cascading to the floor

it was a time before the masquerade
had stalled

ripe from the apple-eyed core, and
spearmint from the winter garden next door

you next to me
as luscious feelings begin sprawling

seed turns to stem
as your eyes bring about a love like burnished
copper

the afternoon glowing, our hearts exploring
as you ask for my hand

it is the love of our story

Veins Full of Sorrow

I bridge today
and tomorrow with veins full of
sorrow

they drip with vital essence from
within

a pattern of light, dark, and the
shadows that mark our heart

tendrils reaching out from the
past

they are flowers rolled in gold
with petals

as soft as the world goes

revolving around the sun
the understanding comes to shore

as we learn to share our love more

Broken Dreams

the sky speaks to me in my dreams
deep and dark

reminding me of many tests

a heart filled with light
and transfigured by design
though

it does make my sins come on slow
breathing into them

I know

it is as it should be, yet it also
reminds me of the snow

that night we fell together
with a mix of feelings
we did think we were part of

some other mystery
intertwined like two trees
perched on the limbs of broken dreams

we always knew
we would come back to seal the seams

and make tomorrow blessed
with all the love inside of you and me

The Ocean's Rocks

the sun rises
as the tide surmises the nature of all the spots
within the ocean's rocks

they wash in
carrying love in all the grains of sand

once held beneath this land
now

dredged up
like a dream
cast to the past

and
bringing forth the present with alacrity,
with a new version of posterity

love forms the center of our poetry

Winds of Time

breaking the earth apart
tranquility sought
amongst the revelers caught

downtrodden all
at times forgotten

the mystery of temerities call
us forward

regardless of the pain we keep in store
and all the love

which we adore
already witnessed in the agony displayed, and
explored

we set sail on the winds of time
and let go of the pain we'd held inside

Moments Grasped

I walk along the sea, wandering
in mind

heart steadfast, like a rope
pulling me forward

and into your waiting hands

in moments grasped
slipping through my fingers
like fine granules of sand

wafting in the breeze
it's all I can do to breathe

into this moment and the next
realizing it's all been
and will be for the best

as my heart opens to the shore
and your heart meets with mine

and two become as one
forevermore

NATURE SPEAKS OF LOVE AND SORROW

www.ingramcontent.com/pod-product-compliance
Lightning Source LLC
Chambersburg PA
CBHW072107110526
44590CB00018B/3344